YOUR KNOWLEDGE HAS VALUE

- We will publish your bachelor's and
  master's thesis, essays and papers

- Your own eBook and book -
  sold worldwide in all relevant shops

- Earn money with each sale

Upload your text at www.GRIN.com
and publish for free

Bibliographic information published by the German National Library:

The German National Library lists this publication in the National Bibliography; detailed bibliographic data are available on the Internet at http://dnb.dnb.de .

Imprint:

Copyright © 2017 GRIN Verlag, Open Publishing GmbH
Print and binding: Books on Demand GmbH, Norderstedt Germany
ISBN: 9783668478015

This book at GRIN:

http://www.grin.com/en/e-book/369472/the-implications-of-the-rentier-state-theory-regarding-the-major-oil-producing

Rebekka Schliep

Aus der Reihe: e-fellows.net stipendiaten-wissen

e-fellows.net (Hrsg.)

Band 2386

The implications of the rentier state theory regarding the major oil-producing states of the Middle East

GRIN Publishing

THE IMPLICATIONS OF THE RENTIER STATE THEORY REGARDING

THE MAJOR OIL-PRODUCING STATES OF THE MIDDLE EAST

by Rebekka Schliep

State and Transformation in the Middle East (15PPOH011)

School of Oriental and African Studies (SOAS), University of London

London, 24.04.2017

AS1, 4816 words

Introduction

The *rentier state* theory has informed much scholarly research on the Middle East and North Africa (MENA) region. A main theorist of the *rentier state* theories argues that "in a rentier state, the government is the principal recipient of the external rent in the economy. This is a fact of paramount importance, cutting across the whole of the social fabric of the economy affecting the role of the state in the society" (Beblawi, 1990, p.88).

With several countries in the Middle East and North Africa (MENA) region ranking among the *rentier states*, it is important to consider the term, which has influenced political thinking of the past and the present. This argumentation raises the question of adequacy concerning the notion of the *rentier state* in analysing political processes in the major oil-producing states of the Middle East. In order to answer this question, this essay is divided into two main parts. In a first section, it will consider the main features that the *rentier state* theorists have set out and the implications that this theory brings about. In a second step, the main limitations of this theory will be elaborated, as well as some of its benefits will be considered.

Close reading of the theories by Hossein Mahdavy (1970), Giacomo Luciani (1987), and Hazem Beblawi (1990), the consideration of critical essays on theories of the *rentier state*, as well as a glance at countries ranking among *rentier states* by definition leads to the conclusion that the *rentier state* theory judges, generalises, and oversimplifies the respective states that rank among the definition of the *rentier states*. The theory focuses on the economy of a state and how a regime manages this economy, and excludes many elements that are essential to the analysis of the mentioned political processes and is therefore very problematic for this purpose. The following section will introduce the theories at hand, in order to take a critical look at their content and fundamental assumptions in a second step.

The Rentier State

Emerging notion of the rentier state: rentier capitalism

When looking at the topic at hand, one should firstly consider the category of rent in itself. Income of rent can include several elements of a given political economy, i.e. factors of production, such as land, for which the owner receives profit without significant input. As opposed to the category of rent, the notion of the *rentier state* makes a claim about the recipient of the rent. A first appearance of the terminology and the notion of the *rentier state* emerged with Marxist writing on the capitalist market in the context of class relations and societal conflict. Here, the monopolisation of the access to and ownership of a certain good gives one part of society the opportunity to accumulate wealth without contributing to the society. This form of *rentier capitalism* introduces the notion of one part of society living off the labour of others while excluding them from their exclusive ownership of private property (Pollin, 2007; Tripp, 2017). This notion brings about a demeaning assumption of a social group being "unproductive, almost anti-social, sharing effortlessly in the produce, without [...] contributing to it" (Beblawi, 1990, p. 86). One underlying assumption of this idea is that the economic system as the foundation for society and state forms the main influence for societal relations and the set-up of a state.

On an international scale, the place of the rent-seeking class emphasising its right to the ownership is taken by the state. With the globalisation of the world economy, the state emerged as the main actor in this equation. A first glance at European imperialism suggests a similar pattern: the claim of exclusive ownership to a good fits the description. With regards to the MENA region, the nationalisation of the oil companies in the 1960s and 1970s led to the state, not a class, emerging as the rent-seeking owner of the resource oil.

With regard to the topic at hand, it is important to distinguish between the category of rent as introduced above, and a set of *rentier state theories*, which have been brought about by a number of theorists and are of main concern to this paper. The following section will provide a brief overview of the theory of the *rentier state*, with regard to its definition by Hossein Mahdavy, Hazem Beblawi, and Giacomo Luciani, to elaborate the main argument to the research question in a second step.

Defining the rentier state theory

Several authors have contributed to the definition of the *rentier state theory*, which is used to analyse the political processes in several countries to this day. A first categorisation of *rentier states* was introduced by Hossein Mahdavy in 1970 looking at "The Patterns and Problems of Economic Development in Rentier States" regarding the Iranian case and the concept of external rent. Hazem Beblawi, too, recognises that rent generally is a reward for the mere ownership of any given natural resource, and therefore exists in all economies (Beblawi, 1987). However, his categorisation goes beyond this, as he distinguishes between "earned" and "accrued" (p. 86) rent, the latter being an effortless income. Beblawi acknowledges that the rentier in its social function is incorporated mainly before the emergence of the oil states in the 1970s. With this emergence, the notion of rentier economies came about, which, according to him, in turn impacted the role of the state in the Middle East profoundly. Beblawi introduced a *rentier state* theory using three key characteristics. Firstly, in a *rentier state*, rent is the predominant income. Secondly, a substantial amount of that rent is gained externally, i.e. sustaining an economy in the absence of "a strong productive domestic sector" (p. 87). Thirdly, this external rent is earned by "only few", or only "a small fraction of the society", introducing the idea of the few versus the many. In other words, if the wealth generation process involves the majority of a given society, the *rentier state* theory by Beblawi does not apply. Here, the majority of the society should be "involved in the distribution or utilisation" (p. 87) of that wealth only. Lastly, in a *rentier state*, the government takes on the role of "the few" and therefore largely receives the mentioned external rent. Hence, according to Beblawi, in a *rentier state*, the government receives its main income as external rent. It is this last point that brings relevance to the analysis of political processes in countries, as in a system with the mentioned features, according to Beblawi, political power lies in the hands of those enjoying economic power, i.e. the few. In this described state system, economic activity is undertaken mainly by the government, and the resulting economic wealth is then redistributed to the population, which lets "citizenship become [...] a source of economic benefit" (p. 89). Here, a hierarchy develops, and results in a relationship between state and society that is based on the distribution of favours and benefits. According to this logic, when taxation etc. are not utilised for the purpose of state provision, citizens demand less in response to the government's benevolence. Consequently, the involved citizens do not earn money as a result of work, but, under certain circumstances, get it awarded by their government, affecting the "ethics of work" (Beblawi, 1987).

In Luciani's writings on the *rentier state*, the distinction between allocation and production plays a major role. This distinction between allocation states and production states is utilised in order to firstly categorise by origin of a state's income instead of the natures of that income, and secondly, the consequent function that the respective state takes in the given context. The allocation state's income is earned from abroad, while the production state's income is based on their domestic production and the taxation. The states' functions are mirrored in their respective terms, with the allocation state mainly reallocating the accrued income, and the production state mainly taking on the function of producing for the generation of income. As in Beblawi's distinction, this leads to a clear distinctive feature in the allocation states' setup. According to Luciani, under the circumstances of a state earning more than 40 percent of their revenues from abroad, and "whose expenditure is a substantial share of GDP" (Luciani, 1990, p. 70), a very different state-society relationship is developed.

In terms of political consequences relevant for the guiding question of this paper, the allocation state features some determining differences. As in Beblawi's essay, Luciani makes the "no representation without taxation" argument. According to this logic, when independent from taxation and the domestic production in general, the state's relation to its citizens and vice versa changes. GDP can be raised by spending and personal benefits obtain priority. As input by citizens is minimal, the notion of "deserving" political rights is absent. With regards to oil, the paradigm of "no taxation without representation" is turned around to this type of "social contract". To take this further, cases of political disagreements are less likely to be made vocal, and if dissatisfaction is attempted to be satisfied, Luciani claims that this will more likely happen to reassure the international community over the domestic pressures. Furthermore, an important point made by Luciani is that in an allocation state, the organization of political opinion is hindered, as a production state offers the infrastructure for political discussion as well as political unions in e.g. factories. Moreover, economic interests seem to be a main driving force in the formation of parties, which are less occurring in a state that can simply satisfy through external revenues. Governments may hereby be "buying legitimacy" (p.76).

Country cases

According to Beblawi, the Arab oil states fit his definition of the *rentier state*. Furthermore, the author adds that the "tribal origin" of these states emphasises the "rentier nature". Specifically, he mentions Kuwait, Qatar, the United Arab Emirates, and Saudi Arabia to follow the rentier system. Interestingly, although Luciani argues that the nature of the income does not play the decisive role regarding the rent, his primary examples of allocation states happen to be Arab Gulf countries: Kuwait, Oman, and Saudi Arabia. However, the author also mentions Libya, Jordan, Syria, Algeria to (at the time of the publication of his article) in some way rank among allocation states. Luciani specifically points out that Egypt and Tunisia do not fit his categorisation.

With the main features of the *rentier state* theories being set out, the following section will outline the implications of the *rentier state* theory as well as emphasise both limitations as well as strengths of the theories, to provide a conclusion on the guiding question "How adequate is the notion of the *rentier state* in analysing political processes in the major oil-producing states of the Middle East?".

The Rentier State Theory as a Theory of State

Implications of the rentier state theory

Luciani expects the "rules of the political game" (1987, p. 73) to be different in an allocation, or *rentier state*. Hence, the theory of *rentier states* has informed much scholarly research on the politics of the MENA region. The use of the theory for the analysis of the political processes in the major oil-producing countries brings with it both distinctive assumptions as well as normative judgments. Timothy Mitchell (2009) recognises how "states that depend upon oil revenues appear to be less democratic than other states" (2009, p. 399). The author summarises scholarly accounts that correlate petroleum resources with a lack of democracy. According to this logic informed by the *rentier state* theory, oil firstly hinders the development of a process of democratisation, but beyond that may even have crushed any democratic features that have previously existed and challenge the development of a civil society. Hanieh (2015) has summarised that the debate around the *rentier state* has focused on the link between oil, autocracy and autonomy in economic decision-making, which ultimately decides which social groups benefit. Some scholars went as far as referring to the theories of the *rentier state* to explain gender inequalities in oil-producing countries. Michael Ross (2008) developed the "petroleum patriarchy" hypothesis, which sets out that the extraction of oil comes with a reduction of the role of women in the workforce and hence the political world. This again is a theory of economic determinism, which assumes that the economic layout of a country influences the political situation exceedingly. Puranen and Widenfalk (2007) state that the rentier economy has "far-reaching political, social, and cultural consequences" (p. 160). In their study, the authors therefore examine whether (as they call it) *rentierism* hinders democracy. The initial design of this research stems from the *rentier state* theory, which suggests the research question. Although the authors reach an ambiguous result, alternative factors are not investigated. Some of the critics of this approach have explored cultural and religious attitudes as explanations for both gender inequality as well as authoritarianism (see for example Norris, 2011). While this approach can also be criticised, arguments against the use of the *rentier state* theory emerge in these critical accounts.

Moreover, one may jump to the conclusion that oil explains the stability of a regime, through the oil's power to buy legitimacy (Beblawi, 1987; Abulof, 2015). The implications of such assumptions arising from the *rentier state* theory have limitations. The following section will present the most important limitations that need to be considered when consulting the *rentier state* theory as a theory of state.

Limitations

A theory of state

While the definition of a state is not entirely agreed upon and the distinction between the state and the society cannot clearly be drawn, it is important to remember the elements, which some definitions of the state include. The term "state" may include groups beyond the government and may e.g. stand for a political community. For instance, by the Weberian definition, a state is a "human community that (successfully) claims the monopoly of the legitimate use of physical force within a given territory" (Weber, 1946). Yet, Gramsci's definition of the integral state includes both the political, as well as the civil society (Bates, 1975). If this definition holds true, the theory of the *rentier state* with its implications applies to more than the government or regime of a respective country. It claims to predict the action - or the inaction - of all elements of the state. After detailed examination of the claims of the *rentier state* theory, it seems that the *rentier state* theory is very broad in scope. It claims to predict the action of a broad group and focuses on only a small part of the actual state, namely on its political economy while other institutions may play an equally crucial role.

Judgmental notions

A first point is closely related to the above-described implications of the *rentier state* theory. The *rentier state* theory sheds a dark light upon both the recipient of the rent, i.e. the government, as well as the citizens of the respective state. With the absence of productivity as well as the absence of the claim to being productive, the government and its people are portrayed as lazy and reclined, while enjoying the decadence that the life off rent has to offer. As quoted above, Beblawi describes the act of receiving rent as "unproductive, almost anti-social" (1990, p. 89), which itself carries a demeaning undertone. Overall, this belief is termed by Beblawi as the "rentier mentality" (1990, p. 88), which is based on the missing link between work and reward. An additional notion of passive citizenship is based on the idea that without taxation, the citizens would not claim representation. At no point does this judgmental depiction of a certain "category" of government as well as society help international or intercultural understanding or the analysis of political functioning.

Generalisation

Another limitation to the *rentier state* theory is its generalising capacity. Even if, hypothetically, the *rentier state* theory was able to predict all parts of the state, it surely cannot predict the nature and action of all states that rank among the definition of a *rentier state*. The term *rentier state* triggers the impression of a single state being described. Hence, theory brings with it the danger of offering an opportunity to lump the major oil-producing states together. Abulof states that only occasionally scholarship on the *rentier state* theory recognises its "heterogeneous and dynamic nature" (2015, p.57). A section above lists the countries, which may be considered *rentier states*. A brief glance at this list suggests the lack of room for variation between e.g. Saudi Arabia, Kuwait, and Oman. While the basis of the economy may be the same, and similarities between the different elements of the state and their politics cannot be excluded, variations are definitive. It is therefore not surprising that the above quoted authors Puranen and Widenfalk (2007) reach an ambiguous result in their study including seven Middle Eastern countries.

Oversimplification

The notion of the rentier in Marx's writing suggests a clear link between the economy and the politics of a country. This belief in economic determinism of economic factors defining most other elements of a civilisation lies at the heart of the *rentier state* theory (Thomasberger, 2013). It is therefore oversimplifying a complex setup of factors determining the different political fields within the major oil-producing states.

To illustrate this argument, it is helpful to consider Luciani's writing. In his paper, he states that "the character and behaviour of state formations is influenced by the prevailing features of economic life in the countries that they rule" (1990, p. 65). Furthermore, he states that this applies particularly to the countries of the MENA region, expressing that "possibly nowhere more than in the Arab world is the crucial importance of the economic foundations of the state as clearly borne out by historical developments in contemporary times" (1990, p. 63). Luciani's arguments are clearly informed by the assumptions set out by Marx and allow for an oversimplification that may exclude a range of factors and explanations necessary for the understanding of the political dynamics of the different oil-producing states.

Through the lens of the *rentier state* theories, the major oil-producing states are minimised to their economic setup, disregarding all other aspects of the respective states. This approach may be relevant for the analysis of economic processes within a certain economic setup. However, while it is impossible to lump together similar economies, as a theory of state, the *rentier state* theory at the very least must be treated with caution.

Historical background

It is therefore important to consider those factors, which may account for the "rentier" features that Beblawi as well as Luciani claim to recognise in the above mentioned countries. Here, it needs to be repeated that each country is unique, and in this context particularly so in their political setup, and in the factors which contributed to their development to this point. A main argument of this paper is that the *rentier state* theory contributes to the understanding of the economic base of *rentier states*, however, in order to complete this picture and to understand the actual functioning of the country, several other factors have to be taken into account. In order to do that, a number of factors may play a role. For instance, the colonial experience, the structures before the emergence of oil extraction to the extent of the 1960s and 1970s, as well as the impact of the international community, in particular by the United States have to be taken into consideration.

In terms of the historical background of the countries under investigation, two perspectives are important. Firstly, the authoritarian structure before the emergence of extensive oil extraction plays a role. Steffen Hertog (2007) discusses the state formation of Saudi Arabia. The author highlights additional factors accounting for the development of the Saudi state to its status quo, such as the impact of the United States and Saudi elite politics, whereas his article focuses on the internal politics of the formation from an institutional perspective. While the *rentier state* theory and much writing "overdetermine" the structural economic impact on the state formation, the author's account adds an important factor to which the *rentier state* theory turned a blind eye. Hertog states that "many of today's permanent features of the Saudi state can be traced back to early contingencies and the crucial juncture of 1962" (2007, p. 556). He promotes the "analysis of elite decisions in state creation in Saudi Arabia" (p. 539) as an alternative to the "structurally overdetermined accounts of the creation of Gulf states", i.e. to the *rentier state* theories. Lowi (2009) adds to this account by introducing the differences in the histories leading up to today's oil states.

Secondly, the colonial impact on state formation in the mentioned countries should not be ignored. The colonial setup allows for an interesting comparison to those features, which are highlighted as distinct for the rentier nature of the major oil-producing states: a system, which is based on external revenues, and is centralized as well as patrimonial, violent and authoritarian (Tripp, 2017).

Lastly, the more recent but very decisive impact of the United States is not represented in the *rentier state* theory. In the above-mentioned article on "Carbon Democracy", Timothy Mitchell (2009), inter alia, observes how the post-world war II political order was transformed by United States planners. A similar transformation initiated by the United States is described as reorganisation of fossil fuel networks at the time of the emergence of the "oil states". Next to the strategic restriction of the flow of oil in favour of the United States, political contestation was strategically suppressed. Mitchell argues that "it was in events such as these that the post-war relationship between oil and democracy was engineered" (2009, p. 411). The author hereby introduces an alternative analysis of the roots of the status quo of the political processes and in this case mainly the lack of democratic development in countries, which were said to have been hindered in their democratisation because of oil. According to the author, firstly, the notion of economic determinism, or Keynesian economy was brought about by Western ideology. This form of obsession with the impact of the economy was not only transferred to the oil states, but also brought with it a way of interpreting the political processes through a particular kind of lens. Secondly, another idea and common understanding is challenged through the author's work. Industrialisation is often times named as the initiator of democratisation, and Mitchell gives an account verified by country cases that explain how the emergence of political organisation in e.g. labour unions was restrained – not by oil, but by strategic repressive action.

Country cases, or "sites of struggle", as termed by the author, include Iraq, Palestine (specifically by the Kirkuk-Haifa pipeline), Lebanon, Saudi Arabia, and Iran. All these sites of struggle represent labour organising or protest and political action that were inhibited by either avoidant action, such as the re-routing of pipelines, or by violent and authoritarian action on the side of the US government or American-owned companies such as Aramco. Mitchell therefore concludes that in fact the "oilfields, pumping stations, pipelines and refineries of the Middle East became sites of intense political struggle, they did not offer those involved the same powers to paralyse energy systems and build a more democratic order" (p. 413).

Counter Examples to Rentier State Stereotypes

Overall, the *rentier state* theory generates expectations of the political behavioural patterns of the major oil-producing countries. The theory claims to offer some sort of predictability of all elements of statehood in the mentioned countries. Hence, it is helpful to consider several cases where the *rentier state* theory did not fully deliver to these expectations. The occurrence of cases in which political action did not match the rentier stereotype proves the points that the major oil-producing countries cannot be lumped together and that variation among these countries needs to be represented, as well as that the economic set-up of a given country does not allow for reliable conclusions on the part of political behavioural patterns.

For example, both Libyan overthrows of King Idris in 1969 and of Gaddafi in 2011 do not particularly match the picture of the detached citizen who does not engage in their country's politics. Furthermore, the expectation of the oil state to be particularly stable or resilient because of its oil resources lead to the expectation of the international community to being able to use oil as an instrument of control. For example, Saddam Hussein's regime did not collapse as a result of sanctions against Iraq as expected by the international community (Tripp, 2017).

The section above discussed the main limitations to the *rentier state* theory, which are key to a complete response to the research question at hand. The following section will shortly discuss the benefits that the *rentier state* theory entails, before moving on to the concluding section of this essay.

Benefits

To adequately answer the research question of this essay, it is necessary to look at the limitations and benefits of the rentier state theory. While several arguments that deem the *rentier state* theory inappropriate were elaborated above, it is still necessary to glance at the benefits it may bring about as a theory of state.

Overall, the rentier state theory may be adequate to analyse the political economy of a country, and how a regime manages the respective country's economy. Beyond that, Hertog's argument on the "telescoping effect" of oil seems particularly plausible. The author argues that the nature of the *rentier state* magnifies the effects that historical developments brought about, which creates the image of the "typical" *rentier state* and prevents change. This logic may be key to the benefit of the *rentier state* theory. While oil is not the only element in the setup of the respective state, oil may telescope particular features that have been brought about historically, and their roots have been explained above. Hence, oil rent and its dynamic can be seen as part of a bigger picture and can under certain circumstances be of help when analysing the political processes of the major oil-producing states.

While Hertog bases his argument on the specific case of Saudi Arabia, the argument may likely be applicable to other oil-producing states of the Middle East and North Africa. Overall, in regard to the *rentier state* theory and its implications it seems inevitable to examine each case individually. Thus, each case should be considered on the basis of case-related historical developments to determine in how far the *rentier state* theory may help with the analysis of political processes in the respective state system. If, as Beblawi claims, "oil has drastically changed the picture" (1987, p. 64), this may be traced back to its telescoping properties.

Conclusion

All in all, the rentier state theory judges, generalises, structurally oversimplifies, and pledges predictability that it cannot fulfil. All arguments considered, as a theory of state, it must therefore be treated with caution. While in some cases, the *rentier state* theory can be a useful element in the analysis of the political economy of a respective country, it is, however, just one part of a much bigger picture. Abulof concludes that the *rentier state* is "more accurately a rentier regime" (2015, p. 57), which comes closer to an appropriate use of the theory, but still does not suitably represent all forms of regimes of all major oil-producing states. In conclusion, the *rentier state* theory may add a lot to the analysis of rentier economies and how a regime may manage a respective economy, yet, its explanatory power does not reach far enough to provide a sound theory of the functioning of either of the major-oil producing states of the Middle East. Studies that associate oil exports with authoritarian rule overestimate causality in this regard and miss out on more informative elements.

Obviously, an analysis of the roots of the status quo of political processes can be insightful. The *rentier state* theory is one such root of the economic status quo, and its relationship of causation to the political setup has been contested. When attempting an encompassing and rich analysis of the political processes within one of the major oil-producing states, it is important to consider at least two essential points: Firstly, it is necessary to look at each country's historical development individually and not to project a general theory onto all states. Secondly, when aiming at a rich analysis, it is indispensable to allow for future developments and changes in the status quo, and not to draw conclusions and therefore expectations that may in total limit the understanding of the political processes.

Especially if the notion of the *rentier state* is used to explain the occurrence, presence, prevalence, assertiveness, or resilience of authoritarianism, and the absence, failure, and missing assertiveness of democracy, the theory fails to meet the expectations of its theorists and may even distort the analysis and understanding of the political processes of the major oil-

exporting countries of the Middle East.

Bibliography

Abulof, U., 2015. "Can't buy me legitimacy': the elusive stability of Mideast rentier regimes.

Journal of International Relations and Development.

Bates, T.R., 1975. Gramsci and the Theory of Hegemony. Journal of the History of Ideas 36, 351–

366.

Beblawi, H., 1987. The rentier state in the Arab world. Arab Studies Quarterly 383–398.

Hanieh, A., 2016. Capitalism and class in the Gulf Arab states. Springer.

Hertog, S., 2007. Shaping the Saudi state: Human agency's shifting role in rentier-state formation.

International Journal of Middle East Studies 39, 539–563.

Hertog, S., Champion, D., 2005. The Paradoxical Kingdom: Saudi Arabia and the Momentum of

Reform. JSTOR.

Lowi, M.R., 2009. Oil wealth and the poverty of politics: Algeria compared. Cambridge

University Press.

Luciani, G., 1990. Allocation vs. production states: A theoretical framework. The Arab State 65–

84.

Mahdavy, H., 1970. The patterns and problems of economic development in rentier states: The

case of Iran.

Mitchell, T., 2009. Carbon democracy. Economy and Society 38, 399–432.

doi:10.1080/03085140903020598

Puranen, B. & Widenfalk, O., 2007. The rentier state: Does rentierism hinder democracy? In

Moaddel, M., 2007. *Values and perceptions of the Islamic and Middle Eastern publics.*

Springer, pp. 160-178.

Norris, P., 2011. Mecca or oil? Why Arab states lag in gender equality, in: Global Cultural

Changes Conference, University of California.

Pollin, R., 2007. Resurrecting the Rentier. New Left Review 46, 140.

Ross, M.L., 2008. Oil, Islam, and women. American political science review 102, 107–123.

Tripp, C. State and Transformation in the Middle East: The rentier state and its implications

[lecture, February 7], 2017.

Thomasberger, C., 2012. The Belief in Economic Determinism, Neoliberalism, and the

Significance of Polanyi's Contribution in the Twenty-First Century. International Journal of

Political Economy 41, 16–33. doi:10.2753/IJP0891-1916410402.

Weber, M., 1946. Politics as a Vocation, Translated and edited [English]. Fortress Press

Philadelphia.

YOUR KNOWLEDGE HAS VALUE

- We will publish your bachelor's and
  master's thesis, essays and papers

- Your own eBook and book -
  sold worldwide in all relevant shops

- Earn money with each sale

Upload your text at www.GRIN.com
and publish for free